RIPENINGS

RIPENINGS

POEMS

JACQUELINE KUDLER

SIXTEEN RIVERS PRESS

Published by Sixteen Rivers Press
P.O. Box 640663
San Francisco, CA 94164-0663
www.sixteenrivers.org

LCCN: 2024911045
ISBN: 978-1-939639-35-6

Cover photograph: David Holt
Cover and text design: Carolyn Miller

For Sasha, Julia, Caden, and Kila

332

There are two Ripenings — one — of sight —
Whose forces Spheric wind
Until the Velvet product
Drop spicy to the ground —
A homelier maturing —
A process in the Bur —
That teeth of Frosts alone disclose
In far October Air.

—Emily Dickinson

Contents

RIPENINGS

The Single Thread

The Single Thread

after "The Layers" by Stanley Kunitz

Perched on Grandma's knee, I warbled "Three Little Fishies"
    to Daddy's always-smile.
Soon chosen Queen of the May, I reigned over the maypole
    in kindergarten,
and having reached the pinnacle of my life success at five,
    sported my Booster sweater at Madison High (as if I ever
    really belonged in the gaggle of cashmered girls).
Saturday salesgirl at Gimbels alongside honey-haired
    Beverly, who regularly pilfered the till.
File clerk at L&T's until, sprung out at lunch, I walked Fifth
    Avenue down to Washington Square and realized suddenly,
    definitively, that I wasn't going back.
Teacher at Jefferson High, three years senior to my acne-
    challenged charges.
Lover in the late afternoons, ears whetted to the first turn
    of a key in the front door.
His frat pin settled on my left breast for good:
    lover   wife   mother.
Babies on my breast now where the frat pin rode so bravely,
    soon bouncing them on my knee and belting out how:

    Down in the meadow in the itty bitty pool
    Swam three little fishies and a mama fishie too.

    Lover   wife   mother

Beginning of the tearful goodbyes—at the corner stop where
    the yellow bus spirited them off to kindergarten.
At the airports, waving them off to their own new-layered lives.
At the chapels, where their brides waited, patient for their
    own futures to arrive at the altar.

Swim, said the mother fishie, swim if you can
And they swam and they swam right over that dam

Lover   wife   mother   widow   crone

So many lives, this single life.
So many me's, this single me,
this single thread unspooling still.

Flashdance

after Merwin

If Daddy had not been commandeered by
Grandma to drive the family to the Catskills,
and Mama had not chosen Kutsher's Hotel
for her one-week break, and Belle

and Gertie had not pushed her onstage to display her
hidden gifts in the every-Saturday-night Guest Talent
Show, her vibrato-rich soprano filling the summer
evening with "A Kiss in the Dark," and the tall blue-

eyed guy in the rear, just leaving, had not stayed on
for all five minutes of her song, his gaze never leaving
her face through the final "wak'ning of love's young
dream," and if Grandpa Jacob had not died one

September day ten years later, sparking my conception—
Daddy, ever dutiful, and after all, the last family hope to
produce the required heir to carry Grandpa's name this
side of the grave—and if I hadn't answered that "Girl

Counselor Wanted for Berkshire Camp" ad in
the *New York Times* that spring and found myself
locking eyes with a muscle-y guy on the tennis court
one July morning, and Don hadn't implored us to spend

three days in San Francisco—*Just three days before
you head back east,* he crooned over the phone—I
wouldn't be sitting here at my kitchen window
lingering over the last coffee on a February

morning, gazing out at the bay and the blaze of
acacia on the near hill, pondering what part if any
I may have played—my dips, my turns, my curtseys—
in this long gambol, this whole mad flashdance of

random possibility.

Presentable

Pandemic, Day 313

How I hated Mama's hands in my hair!
The way she tussled with the knots, coaxed
out each strand, coiled each around a cloth
to produce my Shirley Temple curls—all that
tugging, combing, clucking her tongue in
vexation at my wriggles, my *ouch*es, and later,
when no one any longer cared about Shirley
or her curls, she shaped each strand into braids.
Presentable is what she called it—how we
needed to look to the world outside our door.

Ah, Mama, what would you say to your
Shirley girl if you got one look at her now,
eleven months into lockdown. Fargrinta *face!*
you'd holler in dismay—*put a little color in your
cheeks, for heaven's sake, and do something
with your hair! You walk out in the street that
way?* Well, that's the thing, Mama, I walk out
masked these days—no point to smudgy
lipstick, and no one's looking anyway.

But here's what I'm going to do for you tonight:
Instead of settling in for the next installment of
The Crown on the TV screen, I'm fetching out
the Revlon toolkit—powder, eye liner, blush—

and applying the prescribed disguises. Next,
the neglected elixirs—Arpège, Chanel No. 5, White
Linen: a squirt each behind each ear. As for the
hair, no one's hands but mine have wrestled with
the snarls for as long as I want to remember.

Come then, Mama, let me feel those dear
hands of yours once more—yes, come again,
so eager always to bear the burden of
presentable for me out into the world.

The World Was Jewish

Make a shimel lechol *in the old man's back*
And someone sticks his finger IN.

"Hine-go-seek" we called it,
and as for the incantation to start the game,
its source was a mystery to us, much as the world
was mostly mystery then, except the funny words
we knew for sure were Jewish, much as the world
was Jewish—at least from Ocean Avenue to
Ocean Parkway and four subway stops in any
    direction from the city to the sea:

mezuzahs anchored head-high at every front-
door frame; fathers trudging to the subway,
sample cases steady in hand; the kosher butcher
sweet-talking mothers on the corner of Fourteenth
("For you, darling, I save a special cut.");
grandmas sitting outside the lobbies on
folding chairs, serene as teakettles,
all of it—the neighborhood—buttressed by
the Avenue R temple on one end, the Avenue
    P shul on the other.

News of the world beyond Brooklyn arrived
via the big Philco radio in the living room—

Sunday nights listening to Eddie Cantor, Jack Benny,
and the music of Artie Shaw who, it appeared, was
Grandpa's third cousin (his name was Arshawsky)
and who, in a bold burnishing of the family crest,
    had married Lana Turner!

Lana Turner—that platinum-lit, satin-smiled
sweater girl, who had just vaulted past Hedy
Lamarr to claim first place on my Favorites list—
was married to Artie Shaw, which meant that
    Lana Turner was my fourth cousin!
Except that first-cousin Marilyn, who was
from New Jersey and knew such things, said
that Lana was a shiksa, which meant, she
    explained, that Lana Turner wasn't Jewish—

a small truth that stunned at first, then slipped
in slowly, the way a small pill slips in—one
with sustained-release action that alters
internal equilibriums over time—a general
shift in the body's tectonic balance. It wasn't
long before Lamarr regained her primary place
in my affections, which worked out better anyway,
    seeing as her hair was dark, like mine.

Letter to Henry

I write to you, Henry, as someone
who stumbles through a locked closet door
in her own house to discover not a closet
or a room, but a wing spread out before
her in the darkness:

Regina, you write.
Your grandmother had a sister
whose name was Regina.
She stayed there in 1910 when her sister,
Anna, left; she stayed there in 1938
when her daughter left.

Come, Henry, together we'll light
the *yahrzeit* candles—one each—to the memory
of my grandmother Anna, and your grandmother
Regina, and to Regina's children—

Genia, Lusia, and Milek Sobel—
who perished with her there in Lubień Wielki,
that their names be written in the book of life.

Promised Land

after Family on the Ferry Boat Landing, Ellis Island,
photo by Lewis Hine, 1910

Chin raised, eyes narrowed, measuring
whatever she sees out there, she
stands at the deck, props the bundled toddler
closer in her arms. He beside her, wary-eyed,
bent under the sack: all of home he can haul
on his shoulder tied with string, hand resting on
the small boy in sailor stripes below him—
the boy who eyes the side of the frame for what?
An anchor? A gangplank? A whale lolling in
New York harbor? Only the baby, safe in her
mother's arms, looks out at the new shore
with that naked-baby gaze that asks always,
This? What's this now?

And if I set my camera on 1910, here in
the center of my own lens I find her: Mama,
age six, on the deck of *The Main*, her own wide
brown-eyed gaze, hair pulled back in a blue bow,
a burly deckhand crouched beside her, smiling,
as she bites down on the treat he's shared from
his own landing stash. *Marshmallow*, he intones,
for you. A shainen dank, she whispers.
Traif! Grandma growls, yanking her back into her

skirts. Too late. Too late. Now, *click!* I capture
the moment her teeth sink through the chocolate
shell into a white cloud of something closer to
heaven than she's ever known—her first taste
of the Promised Land.

Legacy

After Mama's morning folding sheets and pounding
blankets, after her afternoon bargaining with
the butcher and stopping at Natter's for an extra
quarter-pound of cream cheese, and after she'd
peeled potatoes, put them on a simmer—all
the small acts of domestic terror supposed
to define her life— she'd ease out of her
two-way-stretch and her nylon stockings,
lie down on her big bed, half-drawn window
blinds flapping in the easy breeze from
Brighton Beach, lie down with a sigh
for a good read: big books in their scuffed
plastic sleeves from the lending library
on Sixteenth Street, books with wonderful covers
of brimming-bodiced beauties and men
whose mustaches stood at full attention:
Gone with the Wind, Earth and High
Heaven, The Foxes of Harrow—from 4 P.M.
until dinner time she'd read and read, and
we'd know to tiptoe past her bedroom door.

But on my twelfth birthday, I'm allowed to
move out of the kid's section of the Kings
Highway Library and into the solemn stacks
where she hangs out. She takes my hand then—

something she hasn't done for a long time—
as if something very serious were about to
happen, and walks me slowly through
the aisles, fingers brushing the bindings
of her favorites, talks to me in the voice
reserved for matters of high state—the dress
I would wear to Elaine's wedding,
or why Aunt Minnie had no babies—
yes, *that* sudden voice, all hush and honey:
Oh, so many wonderful stories here for you.
Here, she says, laying *Rebecca*
in my outstretched palm, *this is*
a good place to begin.

Mama's Answer

Eddie Schlossberg: blowhard, braggart, buffoon—
cousin Rozzie's husband, Rozzie with that wan,
wasted look at thirty-five—the way she laughed at
his gaffes, head bobbing, shoulders shaking
like an aging crone, the time he turned
Aunt Jennie's binoculars around in his meaty
hands, held them to his eyes to focus on sister
Marilyn's breasts: *Marilyn*, he chortled, *hey,*
Marilyn, you look like a goddamn movie star!

And the family turned away and kept talking
the way families do—the way your body comes
to carry a chronic ache without barely noticing it.
Except Grandma, shaking her head later in the
kitchen, would ask the question over and over:
Vas far a mentsh iz das? And Mama would
mutter, *Mentsh? A human being this is not!*

He'd been a sailor during the big war, stationed
somewhere down in the Deep South, and eager
to tell me how they knew how to deal with
the coloreds down there, *the jigaboos, you know.*
That was at Marilyn's wedding, when he took
my hand, held me out at arm's length, peering into
my new cleavage and crooned, *Well, well, you're*
getting to be a big girl now! Eddie Schlossberg—

long gone now, but every day, his face on the front page of the *Chronicle*, his voice on the radio oozing from the Oval Office, and every day I ask Grandma's question: *What kind of human being is this?*
And every day I listen for Mama's answer.

The Sand Bar

I was ten when I first pushed off
from the little kids' surf-rolling close
to shore, longing to join the big kids
cavorting out there, and Out There
seemed like everywhere I wanted to be—
sporting, after all, the Camp Watitoh
Junior Swimmer star on my bathing suit—

so I started to swim   and swim
and swim   but the faster I paddled
the farther away Out There fled,
waves breaking over the bar
barreling toward me as I reared up in
each reach for breath, the sea beginning
to grab me into Somewhere Else—like
the Parachute Jump, but no one there
at the bottom to stop the ride.

And then I felt his arm below me—
Daddy, having leapt so fast from
our blanket on the beach that his glasses,
blurry with seawater, were still hanging
from his ears: *It's not as close as it looks!*
he yelled, cradling me back into shore,
Don't ever try that again!

Well, of course I tried it again, and by
fourteen, in my new bikini, I was out
there all right, eyeing the smiling boys
and looking always to the next sand
bar and the next, all those green lights
beckoning from just beyond imagining:
the ones I grasped to my heart, the ones
that kept retreating from my reach,

and maybe best, the ones that beckoned
me well beyond my depth, when luck
threw out a loving arm below
to gentle me back into shore.

The Amoeba

Was it some reflex abhorrence of
all squirming things that pulled me
back from what I suddenly saw under
the scope, a mucid fleck of will before
my eyes, its bulging undulations? Or
was it something about survival itself—
a glimpse into the engine
of the universe?

In Mrs. Gillam's history class, we
learned about the War to End All
Wars, then studied the one that followed
so soon after, the one our fourth-grade
class had won the scrap-metal drive
for, the year the President died.
The current one was called the Cold
War, and now we crouched below our
desks when the alarm bell jangled
down the corridors on Friday mornings.

In Madison High, we talked about
the brotherhood of man, the *hope*
of humanity, and sang hymns to
a new world at birth, but all the while . . .
all the while on the Bio slide,
the amoeba kept feeding inside
the belly of creation, a moving mouth
that burrowed deep inside, stared back
at us from the skull of the barren moon
and from the cemeteries circling
the night sky.

Up Ahead

for R.B.G. (1933–2020)

We called them *Ruthie*, the many Ruths
who roamed the halls of Madison High,
but not her—she was Kiki, up ahead of
me in school and in every other way
that I could see: one of the coveted crowd,
"the Big Wheels" we called them, and
beautiful she was in her Twirler sweater,
pageboy swinging to the beat of her baton.

Oh, Ruthie, it was too late for me then,
so busy as I was, squeezing myself into
the mold that you went on to splinter, but
bless you for my granddaughters—heads
high, striding down that trail you cleared
for them and armed with the very tools
you spent a lifetime crafting with infinite
wit, infinite courage, infinite care—
tools they'll need to open the rest
of the way forward.

Somebody's Daughter

Like hybrids, we are nobody's daughters . . .
—Jean Valentine

There, lolling in the hot tubs of the sensory
seventies, we learned to *go with the flow,*
let it all hang out, practiced Truth till our
tongues grew tired.

There at Esalen, among the gurus,
the seers, we learned to loosen our belts,
our neckties, our marriage vows, all the
while murmuring our newest mantra:
You do your thing, I do mine!,

and watched them all drift off—male
and female—into their liaisons, the newly
illumined adepts: accountants, teachers,
brokers, house moms—all exploring the
byways of their *human potential.*

But when my turn came, left alone
in the tub with that lovely guy from
Bolinas, when the first easy moves drew
us closer, I—sole holdout as I was, still
mired in the musty old protocols—
trust, civility, fidelity—pulled away.

I'm afraid I'm Minnie's daughter,
I explained. *That's who I am.*

Sister

Jacqueline, *ma petite,* she called me,
a new French word each day from seventh grade.
Ma soeur, she called me, "my sister."
Junie, my beautiful big sister, my nice sister—

the other one too close, too fun to be
nice—and beautiful she was, Junie,
primping in our bedroom mirror, hair
brushed up into a blond pompadour,

sapphire eyes—bluer, brighter even
than my Heidi doll's—a final whisper of
Muguet du Bois behind each ear to entice
the steady stream of Saturday-night dates:

Red, Warren, Marty, Gary, Dan. And Dan
it was. I wept all through her wedding day—
for somewhere between the first of the seven
blessings and the shatter of glass

it came to me that she was never coming
home again, really just a first stop on a long
line each of us would be traveling fast and
far away to one unknown place or another,
and from the first, Junie's line would

always be the Long Island Railroad.
Now once again all these lifetimes later
on a February morning, I pick up
a ticket at Penn Station and settle back

by the window to see the stops roll by:
Woodside . . . Forest Hills . . . Kew Gardens—
the first of her babies, and wall-to-wall—
Jamaica . . . New Hyde Park . . . Hicksville—
the twins and the new split level—

Syosset . . . Cold Spring Harbor . . . arriving
finally at her own Gatsbyland—*Huntington*—
and there she is again . . . waiting in
the white Prius. Two old ladies now,

we hug and then we laugh—
we laugh a full five minutes
as we always do at
the simple wonder of it,
the simple wonder of us.

Homecoming

Seven Reasons Why You Have to Go Back to New York

Because in the corner of the deli on Twentieth Street, two gray men sit hunched over mugs of coffee in arctic parkas talking in urgent, earnest New York tones about flat-screen TVs.

Because here on the corner of Broadway and Forty-Sixth, sixty years ago, you heard that unmistakable family voice—crazy Uncle Moe—spouting scripture from a soapbox. Moe, formerly Moishe from Pinsk, now retooled as a Jehovah's Witness, you on the arm of your new and only love, headed uptown to the Edison Ballroom, your ribboned skirt belling out from the pinched-in waist, so of course, head down, you steer him past Unkie the way you might slither quickly past a door you definitely don't want to open.

Because parents gather at three in the chill wind that strafes the face of PS 11. PS 11—brick-fronted, formidable, five stories high—principal standing sentinel at the tall doors till they open for the kindergarten class, mittened, bundled in hoods and backpacks, bearing today's treasures: the still-wet paintings, the Play-Doh people, the crepe-paper gnomes.

Because in the spring rain you can find the entrance to the Walter Reade Theater on Sixty-Fifth Street at 11:45 in the morning and for the next ninety minutes watch Tanaquil le Clerq dance again—a faun folding, unfolding her long legs in sputtering black-and-white silence.

Because there is a café on Broome Street where the dark-eyed patron saint behind the counter smiles at you each morning, puts up a special pot of decaf coffee, and slides a raspberry scone alongside your cup.

Because on a summer evening at Lincoln Center Plaza, an indigent breeze floats in from the river, riffling silk skirts, neckties, fountain falls, and you have time to leisurely tongue the last nectars of your rum-raisin ice cream cone before the big doors open.

Because a subway busker with a squashed trombone, and yes, a slightly squashed face, happily cadges his way through the crowded car with what appears a surprisingly high rate of return until you see his scrawled sign: *Please, dear people, pay me not to play.* Oh, how could you have ever left this town?

The Parade

June 2018

They are young:
seven young men posing for a photo,
faces fully charged with the kind of
ferocious joy that lifts off in a sudden
flutter of wings and drops you gasping
on another shore entirely.

Ambling a Sunday
afternoon away in late June,
browsing east down Greenwich Avenue,
each corner crossing bearing bigger
news of the Parade: the cheers,
the flash of cameras, the rainbow flags,
the rainbow faces,

and me,
making my way crosstown in the middle
of Gay Pride Day on a Sunday afternoon
in June 2018. No one was gay in 1956.
No one was black or Latino, either.
And women? There were no women
In 1956. Only girls and ladies.

And still, I have arrived.
A random turn on Christopher Street,

and I am here at Stonewall Place,
watching seven young men pose
for a photo, imbibing the kind of joy
delivered in a spate of rainbows.

IF YOU SEE SOMETHING, SAY SOMETHING

I saw something this morning
on the uptown E train.

I saw fifty-two separate lives on
a subway car, sitting, standing,

swaying, sidling up to the closed
doors—fifty-two separate planets,

each revolving in its own orbit,
each replete with its own full

complement of satellites, each
launching its own synaptic gambols:

the girl in the gray flannel jacket,
smiling at her iPhone screen,

the guy just off the night shift,
slumped against the window,

twitching awake with each braked
jolt of the car, the Chelsea blonde

with the Bloomingdale's bag—each,
like me, intent on the errand at hand,

set in the trajectory of what we call
our lives—here in a subway car,

in a city on the edge of a continent
sinking slowly into a great sea on

a globe spinning in infinite space—
and all I can say is I'm no closer to

knowing what to make of any of it
than I was when I first opened my

eyes, except for the certainty
in the voice that echoes down

the aisles as we come to a stop:
Stand clear of the closing doors!

Encounter on the M15

Boarding at Houston Street,
her harangue begins:
*And who do you think you are
telling me where to sit?* settling
her walker under the hold bar
behind the driver, brushing a few
white whispers of hair from
her face.

First Avenue Select heading uptown,
9 P.M.—it's been a long day—
but every day is a long day these days.

The source of her distress, a genteel
fellow opposite, clicking his wheelchair
into lock, explains: *I was just . . .*

You were just, she howls, *you were
just doing what guys like you always do!*

And we, the hapless masked passengers,
asking nothing more than quiet from
a world we no longer know, try unlistening
to the rising voices.

I was just . . .

Yes, you were just! she counters. *When*
I reach my stop I'll let you know exactly
what I think of you!

Well, tell me now, why don't you? he rallies.
I'll let you know when I want to let you know . . .
etc., etc. all the way to my lucky exit at Thirty-Fourth.

And she will ride the next and yet the next
bus, for sure, until the very moment that her
Metro card expires, having found
a way—her own favored way—
of not being alone.

Another Kind of Crazy

Just reaching to open the door of
Starbucks when he pushes out
in a burst of hurry—flash of a man,
fleshy and bald-pated, face florid,

single-purposed, and just as I
calculate the odds of what kind
of crazy—just run-of-the mill New
York City kind or some sub-variety

of dangerous crazy, he stops at
the door, calls out down Eighth Avenue,
Melvin! Melvin, I love you!
Oh yes, I see now—another kind

of crazy entirely—another human
soul crouched in the dark of its
solitary cell. Sprung, ready to take
its one big shot toward light.

Homecoming

After the full-hearted hugs hello,
the teary hugs goodbye,
after the sleety Village streets,
each glazed with memory,

after the requisite visits
to Pablo and Pollock at MOMA,
to Bach and Balanchine at
Lincoln Center,

after the long lunches with Janie
in Lexington cafés,
the soulful dinners with Sasha
in Broadway bistros,

after the 14A, the N train, the
Shuttle, the Air Train, and JFK,
after touchdown and the
taxi to the gate at SFO,

I wake to the peal of foghorns
in my own sweet bed, savor
the coffee and the *Chronicle*
at my own kitchen table—

a homecoming pleasure as
intense as any I've known:
yet one more sign that my
lifelong wander bug has simply

lost its bite, one more reminder
that all my journeys now
are fast heading home.

Passing Through

Sure, there were the gin fizzes,
and our server—Vivian, her name tag
stated—was already setting down
seconds there on the grand patio of
the old Alta Mira, still in its roost
above the bay on a Sunday morning,
and we were only passing through,
ridiculously young as we were, on our
way home to whatever lives

we were off to lead, sitting there,
gazes fixed on the great bay cradled by soft
green hills on the horizon, white spires
of the city rising like Oz from the distant
shore, and the close-in hillside opposite
covered with a mosaic of chimneys
and windows glinting in
the morning sun.

Specialty of the house! Vivian beamed
as she delivered our eggs Benedict.
Hey, you asked, eyes still scanning
the white-sailed sloops tipped seaward
toward the Gate, *hey Vivian, what*

do they call this place we're in?
Why, Sausalito, she answered, glowing
below her beehive hairdo, *Sausalito.*

Oh, Sausalito, you echoed, settling
back in your chair, eyes still fixed on
the horizon. *Wouldn't this be a helluva*
place to live!

White Lapse

Certainly not on *little cat feet* here,
Mr. Sandburg, here on this hill beside
the fabled Gate where daily news from
the Pacific arrives at the continent, heralding
messages into the bay, its first whisper of
fog tickling the tops of the hills for a while to tell
what's coming up ahead. No small paws out here,
not ever, but soon a big swoop, a sweep, a slide
of driving cloud gliding down over the hillsides,
covering the rooftops, burying the city below in
its white lapse of wherever we thought our own
known world had stood.

Invasion

In the beginning they came in ones and twos—
one on the ledge of the tub, two at the drain
of the sink—black and small, yes, small as
the flick of a pinprick, a whisper, but moving,
always moving—a midget ant invasion!
The Raid spray, sure, but soon the pinprick
bands became brigades, and when they bulged
into battalions, the battle was on! Nothing for it
but the big guns now, the ant-trap remedy—
the savory bait that blisses them out, the doom
they carry back home to the colony, bearers
of family genocide.

For a week, as directed, I watched their comings
and goings—the waxings and wanings of their
multitudes—and here (I would not lie to you)
I came to love them a little. I loved the full-
hearted pleasure of their debauchery, their
dedication to bearing their bounty home, their
courtesy waiting turns to exit the grout opening
only they could see. I loved, especially, the one
or two explorers each day, the ones who pushed
out farther in the green-tiled universe, seeking
new horizons, only to die trying, alas, in the
bottom of the tub.

Yes, I came to love them—I, their Attila,
their Pol Pot, their Hitler.

Tiburon Lily

Start any time so long as it's the last
of May, the first of June—and morning, please,
when the hillside waits for you and shadows tease
hollows in the rocks with dreams of night just past.

Best to set a slow and even pace—
whatever you thought you'd come for falls away
in shafts of light that stipple the grass tips, lay
the lower meadows with yellow lace,

and when, at the top, you come to the serpentine,
slow down awhile—the flower will appear,
the one that blooms only now and only here.
Stand still. Breathe. The lily will lean

out to you alone—color of spun
grass, color of rock, color of sun.

Pussy Ears

You won't see her on the authorized
trail here at this west edge of continent,
this green reach of headland held fast
in the arms of the rocking sea.

The authorized trail sports fields of
wild iris, mules' ears, blue larkspur,
but not the pussy ears, no.
You need to walk a ways until you spot
the left-hand path—a thread of a trail
ambling off to hem the edge of the bluff
above the heave and pound of the Pacific:
the unauthorized trail—

and there she waits for you each April—
Calicortus tolmei, pussy ears—
low to the ground, fast-rooted,
petaled in fine fur of palest lavender
(color of amethyst, color of grace),
face turned to the light.

What are you doing here?

       I asked
the columbines, their red flags
fluttering in the stiff sea breeze,
and you, the iris, staking your purple
victory claim on both sides of the
Cataract Trail. You never grow here,
in the woods, but lower downslope
in the sun, in the pleasure of the
green sea meadows. *Oh*, they smile,
*we grow here now—this is where
we grow this year!*

This year! Year of drought, year of
death, year of wildfire everywhere,
smoke blotting out the sunrise, ash
floating from the charred forests—
ash of the ravaged pine, redwood, fir—
all falling on the hibernating soil of this
mountain to feed the roots of the new natives.

What are you doing here? I ask my
Dead—can't you see I'm trying to
write a poem about flowers right
now? *Oh*, they smile, *we're here now
as usual, rising from the ashes as we
always do. Who else do you think has
been feeding your poems anyway
all these many springs?*

Truth

In CERN they sent two beams—
one east, one west—around
a seventeen-mile ring, barely
a sigh under the speed of light,
coaxing them closer, closer
until they collided in a sublime
catastrophe, a constellation
of fire! And beheld at last
the fugitive boson: glue
of the universe.
We have found the truth,
said the man from CERN.

I too saw light this morning
on a mountain trail—
three days of April rain and
each streambed, parched with
a moribund March, had morphed
into a waterfall, each hillside
a firefall of poppies and the trail
a river of pillbugs, a steady
procession underfoot, so
that despite myself,
I delivered death with each
heedless footfall:

poppies, pillbugs, poems—
the only truths I know.

The Long View

Color of mud, color of rust—
tall corpses of pine scattered
among groves of living green.

Charred remains of the Rim Fire
lie downhill five miles behind—no,
this brownout is another kind of
die-off entirely, whole groves of
lodgepole touched by an ominous
autumn brushfire in mid-July, like
cruising through your best friend's
open door to find her fallen, fevered,
reaching for breath—no, these are
the trees I depend on each year,
the landscape supposed to outlast me.

Yeah, she says, setting the lemonade
down on the table before me, *we've
never seen anything like it up here—
maybe fire, maybe drought or bark
beetle—I see more each day*, and
we sigh together as two women
do over a sick friend.

Still, the die-off is outside, and inside
here, the café is cozy, so I reach
for the kind of platitude you find for

such occasions: *I suppose*
Mother Nature will come 'round
again in her own time, and she nods
wanly. Yes of course, the long view—
a perspective good for God
and redwood trees. Little consolation
for creatures like us.

An Almost-Rain

Cancel the mantra and the prayer
mat—set me, instead, on a trail—
any trail for a time. No! Let it be this
trail on a January day in an almost-rain,
suspended between drizzle and mist.

Let it be the kind of small rain that
drifts down from high redwood
branches, barely brushing my face,
each leaf beaded with light, and

I follow the brown path ahead
that lifts and dips along the side
of a west-facing slope. Alone,
of course, my body following

whatever story the trail ahead tells:
story of deep green moss, story of
rain-glow boulders, story of rising
action, falling action—story
with no plot at all.

Covenant

First drops of rain in forever
falling now, falling on our parched soils,
our parched pine, our parched lives.

A bit of sun still muscling through,
and there it is—one foot in the bay,
cars in the overpass above flashing

rose, gold, violet as they glide by—
the other foot riding the towering pine
on top of the distant ridge.

The rainbow—Noah knew it as
the pledge to never end us again with
flood, no mention here of fire, drought,

or self-annihilation. Still . . . still,
always that sudden gladness when I see it—
this shimmering covenant in the sky.

Revelation

For every exile who walked out
of Egypt between walls of water,
for everyone who remembered
the feel of sea bottom underfoot,
the sibilant roar of water rearing
on the right, on the left, someone
forgot. Someone scanning

the dry horizon for a well,
or already mourning the musky
smell of autumn in her father's
fig trees, forgot the hosannahs,
and by the bitter waters of Marah
forgot the flash of dancing feet,
the shimmer of timbrels.

For every proselyte at Sinai,
someone never heard the horns
at all. Someone turned back from
the mountain to bank the fire,
feed the baby, steal a secret
moment with another.

Revelation begins in attention:
While the elders trembled before

the word of God flowing down
the scorched north flank of Sinai,
someone, rising from a last long
embrace, gazed into the rapt face
of the beloved and saw
that it was good.

The Muse Refuses

The Muse Refuses

After the weeks-long assault
on her patience, she simply
demurs, says she isn't
interested in aging, does

not care one whit about
flesh gone fallow or spirit
strutting its impeccable
two-step all the way

down the dim-lit corridor,
says she is indifferent to
vicissitude, except as it
informs a full-bodied

Bordeaux or polished patina
of wear on seven-stemmed
candlesticks. Death
always, or losses restored,

but spare her tales of
triumph in indignity. As
for running downstream,
she is happy to consider

the mouth of the Russian
River at Jenner, how the
edges blur just before it
opens outward to the sea,

how it grows so still.

Mrs. Apollo

My God, he was gorgeous!
the chiseled brow, the curve
of petulant lips, the chest
etched in marble.
I used to watch him
just out of his bath—
each muscle in the calf,
thigh, groin strutting to
salute the new morning,
ready for his dawn spin.

And he was mine!
(which I suppose is what
each of those nine chippies
thought). Bbut let's be honest—
how can you know anything
about a fellow like this
whose eyes could blind you
should you try to see inside?

And now?
I never thought I'd say this,
but I'd be careful of too much
beauty in a man. Too much
light will do you in before
you know it. His kind of
blatant, blemishless

perfection will send you
sniveling to the lower realm

to search for a bit of
the not-so-beautiful:
a flattened nose, a flabby
arm, an open, hurting
heart.

Cassandra

I wanted to know
whose voices called me in my dreams
and where the stars go at dawn,
but more, I wanted to know
what the eagle knows as she rides rivers
of air high above the world—I wanted
to see the landscape she sees, the one
beyond the other side of Now.

From the first, you see, it was Truth
I was after, never Love, and if
you're really paying attention
you'll know you don't get both
in this world.

So when Apollo touched my temple
with that searing finger of light I fell
on my knees before him, not knowing
yet that when a god grants such a favor,
he'll require one in return, precisely
the one I would not give. It was Truth,
remember, never Love,
or anyway the love these randy fellows—
god or mortal—have in mind.

You know the rest, of course,
how once rebuffed, he spat the curse

into the open NO! of my mouth:
Slut! he thundered, raising one shining
eyebrow in a celestial sneer, *You can*
bray out news of the future to your
heart's content, but I'll see to it
no one will ever believe you!

And so it was:
the wile of the wooden horse,
the toppled towers, the treachery
of the queen. I saw it all, I called
it all, and no one now or ever
would believe me.

And so it was and so it is.
Call out the truth all day, my friend,
And see if anyone wants
to believe you.

Tell them. Tell them all about
the plight of the snowy plover,
the great forests in flame, and
everywhere, the seas swollen with
arctic melt, creeping up on our shores,
tapping at our front doors.

Tell them.

Scheherazade

It's about possession,
the old story, how all
the beauty of the world
belongs to someone:
peacocks, peonies,
princesses
belong to someone
and especially to kings.

One wants to see it
as the final triumph of
art, how she seduced
him with song, teasing
the story before him
as one dances a length
of silk ribbon before
a sleeping yellow cat—
just brushing the inside
fur at the tips of his ears,
between the paw pads,
till, eyes shut, still
twitching in dream,
he cannot help
but pounce.

Still, in the end,
in the sallow dawn

of the thousand and
second day, caught
in his great claws
(with all her song
and clever sense),
she was his,
possessed,
and he as well, by
the art that could
only save her.

After

After the first warm touch of a hand
    in the maypole circle,
after the Spin-the-Bottle twirl,
    the first kiss in the closet;
after the arm edging around my shoulder
    in the Avalon balcony,
after the paw-push polka in the back
    seats of the Buicks,
after the first real kiss at the bench
    by the dining hall, my Saturday
    night and all my Mondays on my lips,
after the bedroom adventure that late afternoon
    in December, light streaming
    through closed blinds,
after the cry of the first baby on a
    Sunday morning in October,
after the second, threatening arrival
    on the Golden Gate Bridge,
after biology had had its way with me,
    its frantic fling down the decades
    casting me gasping out into the world,
yes, after the kiss, the bedroom, the babies, the blood,
    then, oh then, is when my life began.

The Octogenarians

I

We arrive at the table in precisely the order
we'd arrived on Seventeenth Street a lifetime
ago: Sondra, the familiar shy smile skittering
toward me, is already seated, just as her
family was already well settled in 2E
when mine first opened the door to 6C—
Sondra, my BFF, my safe harbor for
seventy-seven years. Soon, Jane, radiant
in her lollipop-green shirt, strolls in, dark eyes
still bright with the light that first found mine
in kindergarten—dearest friend, fellow reveler
in the life game. And Adrienne chortles by
an hour late, much as she'd landed among us
three years late from St. Louis (*Well, chop me
up and call me Suey!*)—Adrienne, my rival for
Richie Newman's affections, companion traipser
to the bay, friend pleasurer in the unpaved
world: the great elms along the avenues,
the hush and heave of sea against the rocks.

II
Policeman, policeman, do your duty,
Here comes Janie the American beauty!

A, my name is Adrienne and my husband's
name is Al. We come from Alaska and
we sell apples. S, my name is Sondra
and my husband's name is Sam . . .

She can wiggle, she can waggle,
She can do as she please, but she
Can't lift her skirt above her knees

Anyone around my base is it
Ready or not, here I come

Four coconut Good Humors, please
Four rides on the Cyclone, please
Four junior boxes of Kotex, please
Four tickets to the Avalon balcony,
please

III
With a wide flourish and a wider smile,
the waiter sets four helium balloons
down in the center of the table, returns
with two Chardonnays, one lemonade,
and one Dewars on the rocks.

We begin, of course, with the medical
updates—the bum lung, the unfixed hip,
the squeezed C4, and then, through dinner
and dessert, move on to the real talk, which
like any epic novel-in-progress is multileveled.
Backstories need no telling: the wicked sisters,
the oxygen-deprived mothers leaning out their
windows, the work-burdened fathers trudging
down Seventeenth Street at dusk, bearing
briefcases, sample cases, violin cases.

Nor do the plot lines, progressing tandem
all these years, need elucidation: the first
brassieres, the weddings, the careers,
the babies, the divorces, the grandbabies,
scattered over two coasts, two continents,
the deaths   the deaths   orphaned
four times, widowed seven. No, we all
subtext now—each gesture, each smile,
each grimace sufficient to carry
a galaxy of its own.

Too soon, it's time to blow out the candles,
finish the second round of drinks sent
over by the guys our sons' ages at

the next table, walk out into the deep
evening light of late July—time to part
again at the corner crossroads, our
four balloons floating high
above Eighth Avenue.

Letter from the Deck

on my birthday

Some are already
overboard
and some busy themselves
plumping up the pillows of
the empty deckchairs,
as if to disabuse us
of our losses.

Some stand motionless
at the rail,
unable to take their eyes
from the blue, looming
ice wall opposite, fixed as
they are in the crosshairs
of its glacial gaze.

And some of us
still linger
in the listing salon,
just above the water level,
where a single violinist
teases out the melody of
"You and the Night and the Music,"
and a few glide

into its rhythms
on the abandoned
dance floor.

The rest still gather
at the bar,
savoring the last
remaining smiles
of Happy Hour,
and given the chill
of the arctic
news from outside,

you'd never guess how good
the conversation is here, how
long, how full the embraces.

The Lamp

Memory is no malleable
magic lamp, tempered
as it is inevitably by loss.

Still, we who warm to
its light rub it gently
sometimes, turn it in
our hands as if to
find a way back in.

So I'm listening
to the Weavers sing
"Kisses Sweeter
than Wine," listening
through the ears

of the girl who, eyes
closed, swayed to
its time-driven rhythms
sixty years ago—

the girl who was thinking,
My life.

75% Totality

for Arlene

*In San Francisco, the moon will cover about 75% of the sun.
In Los Angeles, the eclipse will cause little celestial drama with
about a 62% partial eclipse, peaking at 10:21 a.m.*

—*L.A. Times*, August 5, 2017

She'd not been well, my big sister—
we're both older now, warily eyeing
expiration dates—but she's better
today, and she has the special glasses
and the window where we'll watch
the sun shut down its operation for 160
amazing seconds this Monday morning.
But then, it's August by the great bay
after all, when fog lies on the landscape
like a wedding veil, averting the gaze
of the lusty sun.

So there's nothing for it but to start
a drive up north enough and inland enough
to find the bridegroom at the appointed hour.
Past Mill Valley, past Corte Madera, and
well past Novato, talking as we do
all the way, talking about her errant red
blood cells, her sixth cervical disc.
Talking about death beckoning just up

the road. Talking about free will,
reason, and *choiceless awareness*.
Talking about our kids, our grandkids,
our friends all out there riding the
vagrant tides of love, of loss, of fear,
of hope. Talking about why we did
what we did and why we do what
we do.

And we laugh. A lot. We laugh about
why we did what we did, do what
we do. We laugh about the limitations
of reason and we laugh about death.
A lot. And by then we can see above the
hills of Petaluma that there'll be no break
in the fog this morning, that as each
low veil parts, another layer—grayer, heavier—
hangs above it, so what can we do but turn
around and head home. We've missed
the big event, but it's been a good ride.
Not 75% totality, but close.

Magic at My Toes

All those nights before my birthdays,
they tip-toed in while I slept and laid
the wrapped packages at my feet.
Sometimes I thought I heard a rustle—
a whisper of mystery in my dreams—
but mostly the magic at my toes
awaited me in the morning.

Who else has ever known the size
and shape of my longing before I
knew it myself? A purple fountain
pen once, and once a great box of
crayons boasting all the colors in
creation: magenta red, burnt umber,
goldenrod. But even these were
trifles heralding the arrival each
year of the new doll: a first
lightning strike of love, desire,
possession birthed by the glitter
of a glass eye, a painted cheek.

Now all these lifetimes later, after
the long succession of other earnest
gifts—my own *Mary Poppins*,
the cherry-red sweater, the new
Sinatra album, the locket with my
sweetheart's photo, the sapphire,

the cardboard heart for Mother's Day,
the grandma roses for my birthday—
now after this long, singular feast,
what more can I ask?

What more can anyone ask but
that Death, the ever-dependable
friend, will know I'm ready before
I do, will steal into my room while
I'm deep in dreams and lay his
glacial gift at my feet, so gently, so
tenderly, that I'll never wake at all.

Spinning

The spiders are back, scuttling below umber
eaves, riding the eyes of webs. The light
stifled now, lower in the sky, as if a weight
of shadow had descended, and November

takes us by surprise. We'd barely laid
away the magical jabber of July, September's
musing. We'd barely begun to notice the crowd
had moved on, or learned our lines for the somber

masque we appear to have signed on for. How
do we live it out now, our losses accruing each day
along with the falling leaves? How do we play
out the liabilities of November as spiders do,

sailing the centers of their own beginnings,
tending to whatever tears apart? Spinning.

Some days

just holding it together
is enough. Look at the sun
hanging in there overhead—
no ropes, pulleys, just doing
what it does, spinning slowly
through space and time, heft
alone holding it all together:
the planets rounding
their reliable highways,
moons mirroring the same
easy ride, and ourselves
orbiting the rise and fall
of our days, our seasons.

So some days, just doing it
is enough. I pay PG&E,
AT&T, blitz through twenty
sit-ups, feed the philodendron,
and tend to the screen, sorting
the deletes, responds, forwards
with alacrity, and by the time
I look up, it's time for lunch,
time for a friend, a walk, three
calls, and already the sun
is beginning to lower in
the January sky, everything
holding for another day,

while all the while, Time,
that great, patient undo-er,
picks the locks, tumbles
the stacks, touches the sun's
core with the first news
of nightfall.

Shank of the Evening

The plates are stacked in the sink,
most guests already gone—some
best-beloveds among them—and yet
some treasured few remain,

still flush with the flavors of
the more-than-ample feast, ready
to push back from the table, settle
by the fire, the prized vinyls spinning
out the news we need to hear
on the old turntable.

Maybe the best part of the party,
after all, gathering the dark shawl
of the evening around our shoulders,
leaning in toward each other as rapt
listeners do to catch the ending
of an especially satisfying story.

The last low glimmer of Cointreau
in the glasses, conversation riding
ripples of irreverent speculation,
drifting down through eddies of
memory, and Sinatra beginning
to put the moves on the melody—

reminding us just how damned
sweet the last dance is.

A Well-Orchestrated Seduction

for Diane (1937–2004)

She had thought when her time
came to leave discreetly,
no long lingering at the door,
but the habit of living
had grown too strong in her—
in that final year, she'd learned
to settle for less and less:
one sip of a strawberry
milkshake enough to
sweeten her day,

so when it was time, Death,
as was his habit, straightened
his tie, sidled up alongside her,
crooned her name. And she,
always a sucker for a well-
orchestrated seduction,
did turn his way at last.

But even so, he had to press
the goblet to her lips before
she'd deign to swallow.

Apricot Blush

for Jackie (1935–2018)

No, not Eggshell again! she moaned,
taking the paint chip sample from
my hand. *Here,* she coaxed, *here
is what the walls cry out for,* seizing
Apricot Blush from the palate of possibles.
*You'll feel so happy whenever you stand in
the room,* and of course she was right.
She was always right, my old friend,
a true pro: artist of interiors, arbiter
of color, harmony, light. Beauty, her
own North Star, the only truth
that never let her down.

Gorgeous! she'd say, surveying the room.
Gorgeous! her pronouncement on all
life's copious gifts: a flat-out handsome
man, a glass of good Chardonnay,
a choice hunk of salmon, barely charred.
And yes, the Apricot Blush still glows on
the walls of that room where I seem to
linger a lot now that she's gone—as
reliable a pick-me-up as she was, always
with that blatant blue-eyed glitter
and that thousand-watt smile.

Gail

(1937–2018)

The grand old church, the grand old priest
Father Bob, called back from retirement
for this particular funeral Mass—smiling face
full and welcoming as a dinner plate—
Don't grieve for her, he intones, *for sure she is
in Heaven now, yes, at rest in the lap of the Lord.*

Rest? A woman who sieved out each
day's gleam of possibility—a life rubbed
radiant with use. Once, in the Fairfax Parkade,
she came upon a lost woman and took
the poor soul home with her. For a month.
A husband, two kids, two cats, and a big job,
and she gets a homeless woman on her feet—Gail.

Gail, I'd say, *surely you need some down
time, some alone time in your life?*

*Wow, that sounds like hell to me,
that deep well you're talking about,*
she groaned, when I told her how
I need some drifting time, nothing time—
the deep well my lifeblood draws from.

Father Bob, are you listening?
Dear Lord, are you listening?

83

This morning I wanted to tell you

for Arlene (1932–2020)

how they came to me in a dawn dream,
cousins Larry and Helen, to ask how you
were doing. *Oh*, I said, *not well at all.*
She says her only pleasure is falling
asleep. She says she's ready to go.

There they were on a Monday morning,
just as they were thirty years ago—
Helen's face radiant with solicitude,
Larry with that sideways smile of his
that told you he saw more than you knew.

I wanted to tell you how happy I was
to see them—family.
But who will I tell this to? Who will
I talk to if you don't wake up?

Song of an Octogenarian

If you want scrambled eggs, you don't
turn up the heat, no, you beat them to
a froth—no milk, for heaven's sake—
then set the flame low and slow, stir
steadily till they pull together how you
like them. Hard, soft, up to you.

And if you want your impatiens to
hold their own all summer long,
you don't over-water please, no,
just one gush each or you will drown
your darlings.

Pay attention through the years
and you get to see how things play out:
the one great gift that age delivers.

So marriage, for instance—oh,
never easy and often stops working
right. Well then, maybe the software's
jammed, you know, and you just
need to press Restart. A walk in
the woods, maybe, or a week in
Belize just might do it for you.

But sometimes, sometimes, it's
the hardware that's off and there's
nothing for it but to pull the plug
and junk it.   Nothing.

Because love needs all of you, really.
You don't just measure it out in small
breaths, no. You give it all the breath
you've got each day—like blowing out
the candles on your birthday cake,
because then and only then, your
wish just might come true.

Here You Are

for Joel (1932–2006)

How odd that you decided
to come along after all—
I thought we'd said goodbye
that last morning,
but here you are
in the big city, grousing
about the July swelter,
sweat beginning to pearl
just above your upper lip.

Slow down, you mutter.
Are we walking together,
or what?
Past the Brooklyn N stop,
down the blowsy sun-lapped
length of the Bowery,
left on Second under
the lazy shade of sycamore.
We should have taken a cab,
you say. *We're almost there*,
I counter, just making the light
on Avenue A and up one flight of
stairs to see our new grandson,
who bears your name forward.

So here you are, of course,
and how could it be otherwise,
burrowing your face in the
petal-flesh folds of his neck.
Oh, you say, *oh!*
holding him at arm's length,
surveying the new universe
of him: the pate, the puff
of upper lip, ten fingers, toes,
tipped with twenty perfect
seed pearls. *Oh*, you say,
now if someone will bring
me a little scissors, Grandpa's
come all the way here
to cut your nails.

The Blue Car

I'm ready anytime you are, and yes,
there you are leaning against the side
door in your long-patient pose.
Well, I'm in no rush, just savoring
the last sip of coffee, the last glance
at the morning news. After all, we have
all day to get there, and anyway, I can't
even remember where *there* is.
Still, something sober in your tone
up-ends my morning dawdle, so with
one last swipe-off of the countertops
I'm out the door, you already at the car,
but as I start to grab the handle you
stop me: *No, we're taking two cars*,
and I realize that I've never seen your
car before—none we've ever owned—
a blue number, but unfinished somehow,
like an artist sketch of a car, missing a
dimension, and suddenly I'm overwhelmed
with loss and cry out: *No! Why can't we
go together?* but you're already gone,
the blue car drifting slowly down Prospect
Avenue, and I wake weeping after all
these years, the word *together* still on
my lips.

"Spooky action at a distance"

he called it, the great Albert E.,
how two photons blasted miles apart
continued talking to each other
through space and time.

Spin one clockwise, the other spins counter—
send one north, the other echoes south.

"Spooky," this stubborn occurrence he
could not make fit his physics, and
spooky it remained to the quantum
guys who followed, happy to explain

how something could exist
and not exist at the same time,
but couldn't account for this action
they call "entangled," how two

separate specks in the universe
engage in a cosmic dance.

"Entangled," yes, as two lives grow
to become over time, which may
explain how this morning at first
light and waking just this side of

dreams, I stretched my arm to
your side of the bed and, all these
years later, felt your hand in mine—
large, corporal, loving—

I swear I did.

Ripenings

There are two Ripenings
—Emily Dickinson

The first, if you're lucky, comes
on an evening in late July on
the shore of an unsung lake—
children's voices still rippling up
from the cabin, you and he finishing
the last glasses of red wine, watching
Venus light up the western sky—
and for a moment, for no reason
whatsoever, you know you have
arrived somewhere you'd been
traveling toward for a long time.

There is a second ripening, though,
if you are lucky enough to have walked
the length of a long and ordinary life.
It comes on a day dark as the eye of
a storm, a century storm that sweeps
away the outer walls and, all lost,
leaves you crouched in the bottom of
your life—the one room left standing.

It comes with the first knock, but more,
the sudden sputter of joy that leaps
to greet the dear familiar faces at

the door—that small pilot light still
alive inside you, even now, even here
at standby all the while, your own
built-in beacon it seems, ready
to light the rest of the road ahead.

NOTES

"Letter to Henry": *Yahrzeit*: anniversary of a death; Lubień Wielki:
a town in Ukraine, 45 miles east of Lviv

"Promised Land": *A shainem dank* ("thank you"); *traif* ("unclean,
un-kosher")

"Mama's Answer": *Vas far a mentsh iz das?* ("What kind of human
being is this?"); *mentsh* ("human being")

Acknowledgments

My thanks to the following publications, in which these poems originally appeared:

Amethyst Review: "Turning Away"
Atlanta Review: "Spinning"
Blue Heron Review: "An Almost-Rain"
Comstock Review: "Mrs. Apollo"
Earth's Daughters: "Flashdance"
Pure Slush: "The Octogenarians"
The Kerf: "The Long View" and "Song of an Octagenarian"
Tiny Seed Literary Journal: "Tiburon Lily"

"Legacy" was published in *Books Truth Serum*, Volume 7 (Truth Serum Press, 2023).

"The World Was Jewish" was published in *Chapter & Verse: Poems of Jewish Identity* (Conflux Press, 2011).

"Revelation" was published in *Mishkan HaNefesh* (CCAR Press, 2015).

"Revelation" was republished in *Mishkan HaSeder: A Passover Haggadah* (CCAR Press, 2021).

Jacqueline Kudler, a long-time resident of Sausalito, California, taught classes in memoir writing and literature at the College of Marin in Kentfield for many years before her death in 2024. Her poems have appeared in numerous journals and anthologies. Her first full-length poetry collection, *Sacred Precinct*, was published by Sixteen Rivers Press in 2003; her second, *Easing into Dark*, was published by the same press in 2012. A valued member of the poetry community in Marin County, she was awarded the Marin Arts Council Board Award in 2005 and the Marin Poetry Center Lifetime Achievement Award in 2010.

Sixteen Rivers Press is a shared-work, nonprofit poetry collective
dedicated to providing an alternative publishing avenue
for Northern California poets. Founded in 1999
by seven writers, the press is named for the sixteen rivers
that flow into San Francisco Bay.

SAN JOAQUIN • FRESNO • CHOWCHILLA • MERCED • TUOLUMNE

STANISLAUS • CALAVERAS • BEAR • MOKELUMNE • COSUMNES • AMERICAN • YUBA

FEATHER • SACRAMENTO • NAPA • PETALUMA

Text type: Adobe Garamond Pro

Display type: Futura

Printed by Sheridan Saline

www.ingramcontent.com/pod-product-compliance
Lightning Source LLC
Chambersburg PA
CBHW022154080426
42734CB00006B/436